Loie's Disease

A Book about Leukodystrophy

by Maria Kefalas
Illustrations by Lela Meunier

Archway Publishing books may be ordered through booksellers or by contacting:

Archway Publishing
1663 Liberty Drive
Bloomington, IN 47403
www.archwaypublishing.com
844-669-3957

Illustrations by Lela Meunier.

ISBN: 978-1-6657-1567-6 (sc)
ISBN: 978-1-6657-1568-3 (e)

Print information available on the last page.

Archway Publishing rev. date: 1/19/2022

For all the brothers & sisters of
children with leukodystrophy

Preface

This book is meant to explain leukodystrophy to children. The book and illustrations are based on the author's conversations with her own children after their sister – Cal – was diagnosed with leukodystrophy. A social worker, neurologist, and art therapist at the Children's Hospital of Philadelphia advised on the project.

The little girl in this book is inspired by Loie Hammond.

Loie Hammond was the younger sister of Owen Hammond and the only daughter of Matt and Lauren Hammond. Loie lived with her family in Downingtown, Pennsylvania. When she was 2 years old, she was diagnosed with leukodystrophy. Loie loved ice cream sundaes, books (especially *Dogtown Diner*), dogs, and sitting in a lovely garden her mom and dad built especially for her. She was beautiful, brave, and adored by all who knew her. Because of Loie, the Hammond family has worked very hard to help other children and families affected by leukodystrophy. This book is in honor of Loie but written for her brother Owen and the author's older children Camille and Patrick John "PJ" Carr.

This book was made possible with the support of the Calliope Joy Foundation.

Leukodystrophy is a brain (or neurological) disease.

Your brain is made up of grey matter and white matter. Grey matter is like a computer's hard drive where all the information is stored, and the white matter is like the wiring that sends messages through the computer to tell it what to do.

Leukodystrophy affects
the white matter – or
myelin – in the brain.

Most of the time, people with leukodystrophy have inherited a broken gene. When the gene does not work properly, your brain cannot be healthy.

People with leukodystrophy find it difficult
to walk or talk because their brain can't send
messages to their body.

It might be frightening to be around someone with leukodystrophy. They may lose the ability to do things they once could: like walk, hold up their heads, and talk.

Many children use wheelchairs or very special strollers because some children with leukodystrophy won't be able to sit in a chair like other people do. Some kids can't eat through their mouth so they need a feeding tube that delivers food right into their stomachs.

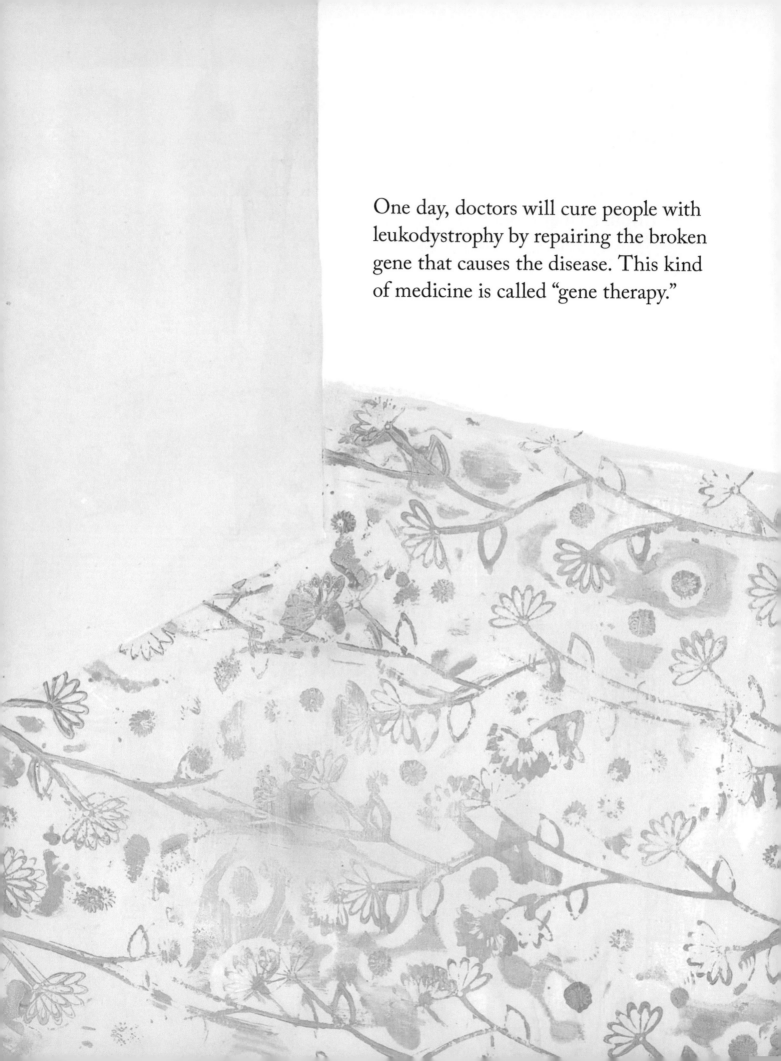

One day, doctors will cure people with leukodystrophy by repairing the broken gene that causes the disease. This kind of medicine is called "gene therapy."

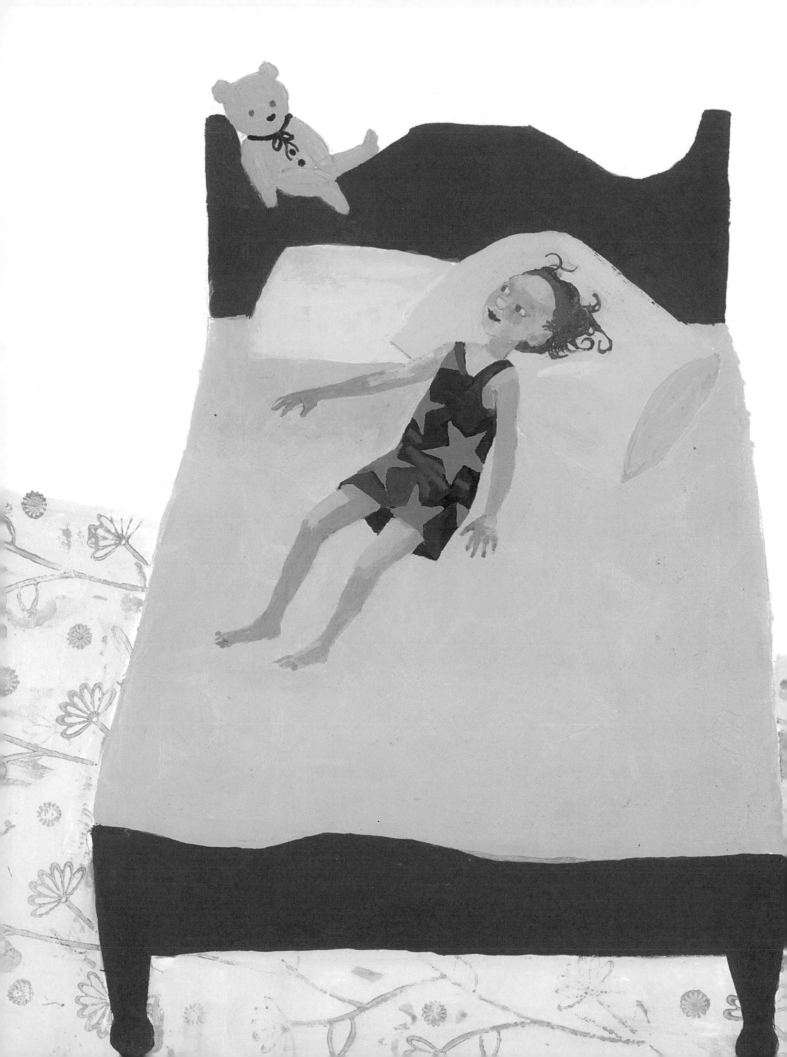

And when you have leukodystrophy, there are still wonderful things to enjoy doing like listening to music, watching a movie, hearing a story, singing a song, petting a dog, getting a kiss, swimming in a special pool, going on a walk, and cuddling with your mommy, daddy, sisters, and brothers. Children with leukodystrophy can smile and laugh. But they can also get angry and bored and sad just like you do.

Children with leukodystrophy will teach
you the most precious lessons of life if you
are lucky enough to spend time with them.
Children with leukodystrophy understand
that the most important thing in the world
is to have people who love you.

Printed in the United States
by Baker & Taylor Publisher Services